Between
States of Matter

Between States of Matter

Sherry Rind

A Publication of The Poetry Box®

Editing & Book Design by Shawn Aveningo Sanders
Cover Photo by Aaron Burden
Author Photo by Jed Share Photography

ISBN: 978-1-948461-51-1
Library of Congress Control Number: 2020930010

Printed in the United States of America
Wholesale Distribution by Ingram

Published by The Poetry Box®, 2020
    under The Poetry Box Select imprint
Portland, Oregon
ThePoetryBox.com

With gratitude to my immigrant grandparents who, by venturing to this country, gave us life.

"Glass, however, is actually neither a liquid—supercooled or otherwise—nor a solid. It is an amorphous solid—a state somewhere between those two states of matter."

~Ciara Curtin, *Scientific American*

– Contents –

Part One: The Distance

Part Two: The Certainty

Part Three: A Life That Big

Part One:
The Distance

Biblical Summer

I long for the days of simple faith
when King Kong and Godzilla duked it out,
stubbing their toes on skyscrapers
and breaking off radio towers like twigs.
Oh, the joy of screaming until we puked.
And then it was over.

They're real enough.
Instead of organic soup,
Godzilla bathed in nuclear muck.
I'd be angry, too,
with those radiation keloids.

Say he wasn't shot off Empire State,
Kong would've gone
like the last passenger pigeon or Ishi
housed in a museum
until death from a white man's disease.

We know, even before the beasts loom into sight
there's always some hotshot
who blows his load and becomes a just dessert
and always a man who says *wait*
and a beautiful woman everybody loves
for being kinder than god or man
and the extras who get trampled—

those would be us.
But we know ways of escape
in helicopters or sewer system or the London underground.
We are as ants to those monsters,
yet we sweep them away every time
and love them so much that we bring them back
so we can win again.

A History of Glass

begins with silica,
that most common crystal structure,
disordered by lightning that burrowed
into the desert and fused into twisted
glass branches hoarding ancient flora.

Volcanoes melt silica to black glass
hard and precise enough to hone into a bison's heart.
The temperatures of transformation
would vaporize us; we are too liquid.
Do not argue.

During centuries of snow and sun
cathedral windows appear to pool earthwards like tear drops.
Although glass is not a solid,
the windows do not yield their structure to gravity. No,
they were uneven from the start.
This is not about you.

The Romans made glass
to see their wine through decorative gladiators and lions
enacting the latest slaughters.
Wedding crystal slips
from soapy hands and exhibits glass' brittle nature—
you may comment here.

Not all sand is silica.
Gold desert sand reddens with the passing
day. Sun glances next morning
on random crystalline sparks.
Not us.

Seneca quantified:
The desire to possess things increases with the danger
of losing them. But what did he know
of that which is already lost,
the wasteland of obsidian when lava cools.

Apache women wept for their warriors'
final leap off the cliff
and the tears fell as obsidian where the men landed.
The women still weep—as do I—
and the numbers of the story's telling are as sand.

Turkey Vultures

In the dip and wobble of their flight
you can imagine how
          to rise on thermals and spiral
      over open pasture, body arrowed
          and wing-tips splayed like fingers.
How boring the sky would be without their stories
with only the strict news
of ducks and geese speeding like commuters
         in one direction.

Mostly, they seem too big for us
too old, in the way
      they stumble on land
      hunch their shoulders
or mass in tiers on bare branches
half-asleep at church

until they raise their heads.
With binoculars you can see those perfect chisels
      elongated skulls with red skin tight to the bone
         beaks sharp as gaffs.

Held close in a photograph
they're Rembrandt's portrait of a figure
robed in gold-brown and black
      the light gilding an ascetic face
      but with a rounded eye, a soft lid
         suggesting kindness in the viewer's conceit

or the truth
of an animal that does not kill
or fight over food
but waits its turn
     one at a time, cleaning
     always cleaning what repels us
         plunging its hooked beak into the afterlife
from which we hide our eyes.

Stones Fall from the Sky

Ten thousand tons each year.
One wobble off course or an accidental congruence
of gravitational fields and
down they go
to be zapped like bugs in our trap
of nitrogen and oxygen.
Most burn away and miss our heads
as we schlep groceries to the car or take out the garbage,
another day overcoming
the randomness of the universe.

Space garbage, like our cells,
carries the strands of its origins,
the primary mess
of dust that spun into our star,
tossing off the leftover lumps
of Earth and Jupiter and meteorites,

some of which hide among the garden rocks
disguised as granite or pocked, melted iron.
If you find a grain-sized rock on Antarctic ice,
chances are it's a meteorite;
but in the ordinary way, it's difficult
to know if a lump in the hand
is trash or rarity.

This perpetual litter has no end in our short sight,
a mass we apprehend no more
than the volume of garbage we toss
into oceans and heap in pits:
boats, cars, plastic rings encircling
the throats of birds, bottles, dishes, foam trays
smeared with fatty remains of supper.

Some of it breaks and reforms like meteorites
but never escapes our gravity, carrying the stories
of our little eruptions
and the long fall through time.

The Fly-Out

This tiny country unfolds
like an origami puzzle
with a carp in the center
swimming in water miraculously
not wetting the paper.

The country is paper.
The unfolding makes room for birds
visiting from far places.

Some stay for a season;
others exchange news and pass through.
Some die; some return next year.
I try not to touch their lives.

They have no borders
but in spring they stake territory
with voices, different songs
saying *mine mine.*

Even the youngest,
bald and blind, do not soil the nest,
shuffling up to squirt droppings
over the edge

of twigs, moss, hair from dogs
folded tightly together into a cup,
a tiny country in the pit of a branch—

then they leave behind
everything collected,
while I keep so much
glass or paper, water or rock,
heart circling like a fish caught in a bowl.

The Distance

Now the summer heat and light stop
beating at us and cutting
knife-edged shadows across our eyes.
They turn kind, like a friend's palm
on the shoulder, bodies fitting
side to side, facing the spreading dark.

From where I sit far out in the lake
swaying to the heartbeat of gravity and current,
I hear a woman's voice rise like a sparrow,
a man's voice rolling below, detached
from the diorama of their picnic.
Pictured from shore
I am a rowboat with a figure in it.

I remember standing on land
beside a wood table, cutting irregular lines
in a pan of cake. My son pointed—that size,
the biggest because he was little—
and I worked it onto a plate. More,
for the children, my cousins, my husband.
I licked my fingers, laughing
and now hear the wispy tail of the sound
eddying from shore

where the little figures pause
in the moment before anything
might happen—a kiss, a downpour, a death.
I watch their dissipation in the last of the light,
those people who might have been mine
a long time ago.

There Will Be No Revolution

~with words borrowed from "The Revolution Has Ended"
   by Adam Zagajewski

All day, explosions rumble from the gun range.

Hunters honing their scopes for deer season
shatter paper silhouettes.

The leashed dogs and pedestrians march
up the street, inured to the crash and rumble
of transport trucks charging over the hills.

The wind has shifted, blowing off wildfire smoke

and bringing rain like pebbles on children
peeved as always, shouldering each other
at the bus stop, the mothers changed
from summer dresses to hoodies,

the victory of loading children each day into school
and packing them home safe.

They believe life has restrained
its tendency to darken with the season;
they stop listening to shrieking headlines.

No weapons can leave us victors or vanquished.
Down the street, an old woman sits in the café and cries.

This Time of Year

everybody's making holes

the chicks scratch through their litter
only to find yesterday's news beneath

the flickers peck the earth for ants
and enlarge their home in the alder

my nephew's son cries out
when every hole in the bath fills up

I dig post-holes for the new fence
and little divots in a row for peas

and tiny needle-holes
across the sheer fabric of a summer dress

and my heart dissolves
in the space between your coming and going

The Moment He Leaves My Hands

My fingers cup around a puff of air
with a beating heart
        and slowly open
like this, my hands say, every life begins
at a still moment when all breath is held
        until the burst
of red flame where sunlight strikes the ruby throated
hummingbird throwing himself
up against the weight of air too quickly
for human eyes to track,   he's rising
he's gone
a mere thickening against the sky
but my hands remember
the infinitesimal weight and heat
of that bird as if I, too,   could transform
if only I were quick enough.

Sea Turtle at Tortuguero, Costa Rica

"There is grandeur in this view of life, with its several
powers...."
~Charles Darwin, *On the Origin of Species*

Blind, we cross hand to shoulder,
one on one, only our guide knowing the way.
The dark is a tent dropped on my head,
the air a deep bath and my body, gills.
Cautionary whispers float down the line
log ahead, rock, dip
until we pull up in a circle
and our eyes relax into the night.

The sky's damp cotton batting
bleeds indigo into the sea.
The sand has turned to slate. We are as quiet
as the womb, remembering
our own children newly planted
and even then not quite ours. The hushed surf
fills our ears and chests like heartbeat
until *she's coming* breathes along the line.

Our view of life is half imagined
as Venus rises, climbs to dry sand, and begins to dig.
But there's something she doesn't like—
a root, the texture of sand, this night—
or she just feels it's not the time.

The rumor ruffles again—*she's going*—
but all we see is the torn surface of the sand
until she nears the water line
where—*there*—the dark intensifies
in the shape and weight of a boulder.

[...]

Now we feel the labor of each inch she hauls herself
pushing in the front flippers, heaving earthbound forward.
She rests between worlds as if, like us,
she has almost grasped the order of things
but then the waves lift.

Achilles' Horses

Zeus saw the tears of those immortal horses
spattering dead Patroclus
and said, "What was I thinking,
giving you to murderous Peleus
who handed you off to his berserker son?
Oh, well." Zeus returned to his own entertainments,
leaving the horses

to Achilles' whip.
Three times around Patroclus
the panicked animals ran from the stench
of blood and guts, Hector's corpse
rattling behind the chariot. They ran
fast enough to meet Achilles' spittle
coming the other way.

Everyone died
but the gods safe in their high-rises
and sea caves. Abandoned on the mortal plain
Balios and Xanthe, harnessed to plows,
the gold Anatolian dust mud-hard on their flanks,
turned Greeks and Trojans into the soil
and bronze arrowheads out. The smell of human rot
never left their nostrils.

Though easily spooked
and no longer reliable, they geared up
and carried men into every war
for the next thousand years
while crops and walls of Troy rose again
and fell in earthquakes and fires without epic
heroes to raise the horses' spirits. They stopped loving
any of us.

[. . .]

When the last families, illiterate
and verseless, plodded into the hills
and sand filled what was left of the palace,
the lost horses, offspring of harpy and west wind,
faded like tracings on a cave wall,
kicked at the doors of the underworld
begging to be let in.

Linnaeus Names Andromeda

Andromeda polifolia

By the time he reached her
he thought the mud was talking

He couldn't remember warmth
and here was this pale pink flower

Gazing downwards, belled petals the blush he fancied
on *a virgin of most exquisite and unrivalled charms*

In loneliness, illusions
bog plants anchored but floating

Water licking at Andromeda's feet
and the dragon a salamander sullying her pristine skirts with
    mud

All preparation and waiting, all uncertainty, her pulse of color
growing paler and paler till it withers away

The Days

when you lived, August
was a delicious bruising
the aftermath of riotous sex

bringing the multi-layered perfume of blackberries
a complex and fleeting birdsong

you built the trellis where scarlet blossoms gave way
to beans with a sway and whisper
of pliable wind chimes

my skirts, the leaves
my rhythms, the click of a stem
the hushed slide into the pot

now tomatoes turn hard red with effort
and sterile blossoms drop from the squash
lilies release their petals one by one to the fire

as the plants betray their promises, the fibers
of my skin and muscles fray more each year

August could go anywhere
the light undecided between cloud and sun
days promise nothing but their end

my shelter is built of corn stalks
where you used to stand
the wind hisses through

Tell the Bees

When I hover in the bee traffic
beside the wild rose, the lavender and sage
grown into a bulkhead
along the walkway,
the vibrato's a cloud around me
and I hold so still that the magnified thrum
of a hummingbird sweeps into memory
before I realize the bird flew past my ear.

I planted without understanding
what was to come.
Drunk on roses, I might believe anything,
Conan Doyle's fairies and séances
as if the dead were hanging around
waiting for a call. I confess
to one-sided conversations.

The bees sound a warning
not to interrupt their concentration
with my household news—
the dog chewed a pillow;
I gave away my husband's last shirts.
They tell me the plants are rich
with the pollen I've nourished
and they are taking it home.

The Newly Bereaved Fixes a Toilet

Mend the broken threads before the whole seam gives.
Assemble all ingredients and clean as you go.
Don't put your hand near the mangle—
the girl up the street wears a hook.

Never throw away old parts until you know the new ones work.
Always put your tools back where they belong.
Don't put your hand in there;
it's filthy.

Fix a leak before there's rot.
Mend a part before it breaks apart.
If you put that on your hand,
you're his.

He leaves three socket sets
and two chain saws.
I cannot find a wrench.
Wrenched, wretched, retch.

The chain is always the first to go,
a matter of rust and a simple fix.
See what happens
when you let things go?

Flappers distract from the task at hand:
ducks readying for take-off,
beaded dresses, bobbed hair, t-strap shoes.
I will never dance again.

Today we have the naming of parts:
float, valve body, float cup, a fill valve
worn by years of joyless repetition.
Once undone, there is no going back.

With the broken pieces of my household
in hand, it's sink or swim.
Therefore choose life
and the Talmudic discussion on the package.

I insert the valve, washers, nuts, and bolts
and am so astonished that the toilet flushes and fills
and does not leak that I press the handle again
and again, *wasting water, spending pennies*

without a thought
for what has passed
or is present or cannot be.

The Body Falls Away

"...as the body then falls away from you."
~C. Dale Young

                    More of a slippage—
imagine a scull drifting
from the dock when he neglected
to check the knots.
                    The breath slows
to little sips
and red cells flatten for lack of oxygen,
his body falling away
                    yet not away
in an illusion of motion
without progression,
                    like the ripples
appearing to stay in place
on the lake's surface.
They flatten and fade
                    with distance
to the opposite shore—
an Impressionist painting
of a rocky beach
                    slapped by the same
waves that will claim the fiberglass scull
if no one hooks it back in time.
It falls, it was falling,
                    it keeps falling.
You can catch a boat or body
but the breath slips away,
pulling shut the organs
                    one after another
behind it. The pink wash fades
out of his face
                    from life

to memory to the imagined
temperature of his hand.
                    He is dying again
today, with the perpetual motion of waves.
Distance fades only the vision,
not the illusion of the body
                    drifting away from me
and never landing, his sentence—
his answer to me—
                    unmoored

Blue Shirt

As a child keeps a scrap of baby blanket pinned in his pocket
I keep a square of your blue shirt,
worn to lace these eighteen years without you in it,
pinned to my bra strap where you can brush my skin.

Nothing else touches me, not other men or good luck charms,
not the flowering plum or pictures of puppies—
our dog was one post of our unit
as we dug the garden and fixed fences
through all the staggers, stops and restarts of living.

When people ask what happened, I tell just a scrap
because the truth wriggles and shifts
like a Proteus never to be caught
in the waves that dragged you under.
I swear I was beamed into another dimension

where the wrong life plays out in a strange house,
the trees gone and our son replaced with a robot.
I myself have grown unrecognizable
without you to be my mirror. There is no one
to tell me not to be afraid.

The remaining birds have quieted; every few years
I hear your voice rumble out of a box.
I can't see you clearly, but sometimes you look at me
from a place under water, blurred with fallen leaves
where only the blue plaid shirt is true.

If I Could

If you could share a private meal and one-on-one conversation
with any person whether from this time or another, whether
real or imagined, who would you pick and why?

Unlike that wimp Orpheus,
I'd haul my husband back from the dead
with muscles hardened from lifting
bags of dog kibble and chicken feed,
from pruning trees and wrenching pipes,
climbing, pounding, plus the scrubbing
of hidden dirt he never gave a thought.

I'd take him to a grill because I still can't cook a steak
to save my life, the delicate balance of charred and raw.
Order thick and bloody, you'll know you're eating
something once alive.

And why, you ask, sit across the intimate table
and listen to the same old stories—there's nothing new
from the land of the dead—I tuned out
years before he died?
We might discuss that quicksand feel
of never keeping up with things that break,
him tossing quotes from *Tristram Shandy* and *Huck Finn*
as if words stopped a leaky roof.

I'd come 'round to asking why
didn't he save himself
and of course he'd say he tried but couldn't
and I'd say look at your son, he needed you here
to make him keep going at life
because he never listened to me any more than you did.

[...]

And I wouldn't be able to stop
any more than my husband had stopped.
He'd pour another drink
and I would burn.

Oh, my crass and selfish nature
I'd do it again and again
because he loved me.
I'd say *eat slow*.

Storm Season

During a pause in the November storm
I'm safe to go upstairs with the skylights or even outside
but I stay in the kitchen
and watch juncos settle to the deck, fan out
and zig-zag across parallel boards, pecking at twigs, litter,
the storm's smorgasbord of mystery foods.

In the market overlooking the Sound, where my grandfather
    sold fruit,
people will hurry from the shelter of restaurants
to gather their apples and lettuce before wind drives in the next
    rain.
Last week in a desert market, the scarves and bracelets,
oranges and tomatoes, arms and feet
stormed into the air and down.

Having migrated like a bird across the world,
my grandfather stopped at the far edge of his new continent
where the water was like home.
In puddles where they dip pearl-pink beaks,
the juncos' black hoods ripple back at them.
I wonder where they sheltered
when wind-ripped branches from the poplars speared into the
    ground
and whole fir limbs crashed on my roof.
I wonder where my Parisian cousins spent Friday night,
if their grown children gathered to light Shabbat candles
or if they went to cafes or concerts.
And if they came home.

The juncos bounce like wind-up toys
and lift off as the towhee, another black-hooded bird,
parts the vines curtaining the rail.
He pokes at mossy cracks and dives

[. . .]

over the side where wind and wing catch him up.
He can't fall.
I met them once, those cousins
whose parents, after the war, returned
to a country that wished they had not.

The little sparrows sweep through
to pick the last bits of food
as if all the birds had planned our choreography
of touching down and rising up.

New Year's Eve

When thunderous echoes
from the gun range merge
with blasts
carrying over the neighborhood
from the little park
where everyone gathered last summer
for picnic dinner and a local band,
where now the vandals crouch
with their illegal gunpowder
and set off malice
and uproot the trees,

I consider the broken strings
in my life; in a quiet unknotting
like shoelaces parting
from each other, those
with whom I entwined
have fallen to time and age.

Finally there is a pause,
not of quiet but the waiting
while a congregation bow their heads
and prepare to recite
the incantations against evil,
when the great joints of the earth
begin to shift against their sockets.
All our work will be undone.

Properties of Glass

Nothing stays at rest

molecules of a crystal—table salt
snowflakes, diamonds, quartz—repeat
their patterns in tight formation

like a platoon at inspection
faces still as glass but young
and like glass, not organized

a state between two states
neither liquid nor solid

only light slips through the empty spaces
glass shows true or changes light's direction

with its imperfect curve

silica becomes glass
forces moving across a desert feel
heat's random motion of molecules

when the bonds break rank, silica discards
its crystalline structure and matter transforms
bodies burn, glass melts

the gather of glass burns its own light
until it cools, hardens
never returns to its former state.

Slip

I saw him through a window
in blue-gray light of dawn or dusk
leaving distance shadowed and the near
uncertain. Moonlight
or rain washed him silvery,
even his face metallic
as he carried across the yard a young tree and shovel.
"Not too close to the house," I called
but of course he couldn't hear
for the wind loud as thunder
and the rain arrowing drops
like sparks in the reflected light.
Just home from work, clad in a suit
and hiking shell, he began to dig
near a tree we had planted the last spring
for a line of fruit between house and black woods.
I sat alone at a table,
half to the cold window-side,
half to the warm house
and woke to the false dark
of winter morning when rain beats out the rising sun,
and hungry dogs bark and paw at my door.

The Misnomer Renaissance Faire

The Airedale woke us, crashing and howling
against the door. John and I watched a coyote leap the fence,
its gold melting into the dark wood
and our hen a limp ribbon in its teeth.

The dog tracked scattered chicks
we picked like cotton balls and stuffed
under another hen. Chickens forget their history overnight
but we told each other the story over years.

> I watched him fade to dark.
> Our revels ended, our history
> mine alone to stage or improvise.

In this summer's Renaissance,
Death wears a white mask, gives candy to children.
There's less mud than the olde days
but everyone's wearing the same puffy shirts
and wads of skirt brushing the cow pies.

When the hens' jester hats slip down their heads,
crows disguised as ravens get the crumbs.
Not every child gets lucky
at the trout pond. In warm water,
the fish lose appetite, go flaccid.

> In the hospital aquarium, fish refracted
> bigger than life, brighter in full-spectrum light.
> Someone cleans up the bodies.

Time refracts everyone's history;
every marriage, a reenactment.
The singing pirates in real beards and gold earrings
don't know jib from jibe.

July transforms from rain to heat.
The lettuce bolts, the peas collapse and dry,
Death steals their rustle.

> Time fills with belled hats
> and dancing to pipes, ribbons unfurl
> behind our little lives' darkening mirage.

Adaptation

My ambition was to pause every week
when hauling the garbage can to the curb

and look up at the sky, whether cloud or moon,
maybe a lucky meteor burning across the dark
like the industrious angels climbing and descending
their never-ending ladder to nowhere

and I would return to a never-empty house.

Some people adapt quickly like the rat or coyote
learning to appreciate bread without butter
and reducing wild leaps to safe puttering.

Some, like a whooping crane, rely too much
on one marsh and refuse to eat anything but favorite
invertebrates.

I will never get used to this

yet even now
when I let the dogs out in the evening and lean
across the porch like a figurehead sailing

into a night sky still washed with light
behind the black-green lace of trees,

when the air passes
like an owl's wings through my arms
for the barest moment, I accept.

Part Two:
The Certainty

Your Early-Morning Videos

The day crouches on a ledge.
Inside your apartment, you focus
on cats' padded paws
and wish you could leap sideways,
startling everyone.

The cats' ears enact whole conversations
and flick-switching tails work a random code.
One of these days, you'll crack it.

Humans kindly absent themselves
leaving only a hand jiggling a feather, a springboard lap.
You like that every kitchen's laid out much the same,
the family room carpets ranging beige to brown,
America on a slow day recording cats.

You almost feel the rapid calculations streaming
through their bodies before a leap.
Sometimes they look chagrined
at a pratfall, pausing with heads lowered
and maybe a quick glance at the camera.
Who is watching?

In the background, low laughter
at a cat clawing a bag stuck on his head.
Someone will be scratched.

The cats practice their neck-breaking pounce
on mechanical mice, yarn, lights played across the floor
until, bored with hunting,
they drop like the dead
in their safe houses. Still,
you follow the promise—
you'll laugh until you cry.

Tuning

Amid the songbirds' multi-hued notes
one squirrel mutters
like my great-aunt's adding machine spitting out pages
per per per piss. When the tiff ends,
his sums equal zero.

The birds—there must be some orchestral
practice today—send a different melody from each tree;
the crows and jays, with their shrieks of morning news
and commuter pique, go quiet
leaving the air to tanagers and thrush
rising over the tenor tuba of a dove

in a fugacious chorus
like the smell of lilacs, alive
only two weeks in a year.
The dips and flutters of sound fall off

to one line, one bird
who keeps punching
out the notes until the answer's right.

How to Choose A Lawn Mower

It's not love that calls me to the things of this world
but the lawnmower wobbling dulled blades across the years.

A good mower, I'm told, should last a lifetime
like a good marriage, with yearly tune-ups.

The mower followed me from house to house
sometimes leaving a screw here, a nut there.

It made constant demands—the salon refurbishment,
the putting in and taking out of gas and oil

until I traded it for a push mower.
Now I supply the power

the glory of grass stems whirring around my legs
the handfuls of soft blades I shower on the hens.

Reseeded Lawn

"Your prefrontal cortex—where the concentrating and
deciding gets done—has been shrinking for some time...."
~Gerald Marzorati

I could buy the sprinkler that waves forward and back
like the Queen tipping her hand to the hoi polloi

or an American style swearing and spitting
so hard that it spins itself

or a fairy-circle fountaining like a lily.
My life has choices and nobody

telling me squat. With my shrinking cortex unable to decide—
there'll be no growing and certainly no flowering—

I thumb the hose and dampen the mulch to
my favorite shade of chocolate.

Most of my allotted time having passed, I might as well stand
like a cow, empty of thought, my sweet dark eyes

contemplating the yard where the weeds used to be,
certain, by dint of experience, something will come back.

Miss Sarah Stone Records Natural Curiosities from the New World, 1783

"In the evening, where we pitched our tents we shot two crows
and some loraquets, for supper. The night was fine and clear...."
~John White, Esq., *Journal of a Voyage to New South Wales*

Miss Stone wished for an anatomist
who knew how skeleton and muscle tied beneath the skin
in particular the curvature of the neck—
these explorers who shot and stuffed
the specimens with cotton batting
always ate before recording.

Not having seen the gum trees where lorikeets spend their lives
among the grey-green leaves and silver branches,
she posed the bird on a brown English stump,
its breast thrust forward and head high
like a ship's figurehead,
the wings and tail fanned,
ready to fly. She lined
each feather in fine black ink,
surmised the color of the empty sockets,
shaded the vermillion face to the faded rose
of an English bird and dampened the back's iridescent green.
In life polished like a gentleman's shoe
the black beak curved true but pale.
What else would she know?
Inside the museum, she painted
to keep alive, not the bird but the knowing of it.

Everything mattered: the number of spines
on a beetle's legs, the meditative face of a tube-nosed bat,
each featherlike branch of a Gorgonian coral

[...]

and the shadows beneath, as if they lived in light.
She perched a Grey Goshawk on the side of a mountain,
head in the sky. The White Gallinule on a rocky shore,
served in too many dinners, now extinct.
When the Leverian broke up, specimens scattered
to anonymous collectors and tossed in drawers
with pens and children's rock collections,
the colors Miss Stone mixed
survived like fossils: mineral, undecayed.

Sarah Stone Paints the O'o Bird

Lever Museum, London

From Cook's Hawaiian plunder
Miss Stone extracts a red and gold cape,
sketches the folds, hints
at the eighty thousand birds
plucked for a king.

In her hands, shadow's the illusion
of lift and heft, a feather's weightlessness;
color's the clue to every mystery—
how a touch of moss brightens the red
and the hidden gold
of an olive-brown bird becomes a cloak.

Below, she replicates the tattered bird.
She adds a white hair-stroke along the iris
suggesting the infinite patience of animals
who know their fate. The O'o's beak points
to the cloak, its eye at the families
strolling through the short-lived museum.

The cloak whispers as the feathers shift
against each other, simulation
of a bird lifting and ruffling its feathers
to hook a million tiny barbs into place.
Miss Stone smooths the page before the long sleep.

Norway Lemmings

At first we believed lemmings rained from the sky
plopped gently down and ran to their burrows under the snow.

When they poked out their heads to scold our passing feet
we plucked them from the earth like potatoes.

Centuries on, the Disney crew tossed them into a river
to spread a myth about mindless dispersal.

Lemmings conduct most business under snow crust—
eating moss, dating, birthing large batches to feed the foxes.

In these warming years, there's more water and less snow.
Mud is no place to raise a family.

Hungry foxes shift from lemmings to shorebirds;
owls starve; nests fail.

Now *Time* lists lemmings among the year's influencers
the hand that jerks the chain from the bottom up.

The snow's fat, wet flakes run into the sea.

Primate Study

A door opens to the other side,
a flurry of monkeys,

a swaying branch, an apple slice falling.
Silver-white and black slip through the green.

We are heavy in coats
in fermenting vegetation, soupy smells.

When faces emerge in the glass, we unlink the puzzle
between light and reflection.

An olive shoulder, a white-bearded elder
with hooded eyes, a baby worn like a scarf.

Children hop, cross their eyes, stick out their tongues—
look at me, me, me—wait

for a monkey to splat excrement
against our glassy selves

but we're boring. They groom each other
heads bent to backs, fingers minutely sorting.

We quiet. They reach hands and feet slowly
as if through water. They come down to us.

Wildlife Rescue

A woman—it is always a woman—
scooped this resentful heap from the base of a tree.
Now he has a private suite, mesh-draped
to hide the sight of human faces.
He hunches in his fug of meal worms,
chopped grapes, kibble, and smelt heads,
Aegean-blue eyes a talisman against us.
Caretakers say he's cute.

We are above the law
of nature that declares a baby dead
when it falls from the nest or loses its mother,
but we have rules: love all, touch little,
mourn no one, do laundry.

I pick up a grape with the tongs, tap
the side of his beak; let me in.
I'm a mesmerist circling the grape around his face;
he sees the shadow of a parent swooping down
and the beak opens as wide and deep
as a post-hole, sounds bubbling up
even as he swallows, flapping his wings
for more. I'm shoveling fuel
into the voracious furnace, up to the shut-off line.
He sleeps while cells divide and multiply
and the creature shape-shifts into a glossy black
hellfire deacon.

We move him to the teen street gang
perched in the rafters of an old horse stall
where we leave their meals, bowing our heads from sight,
and never speak.

Once they light out for the cedars,
they'll listen only to the clicks and caws
of other crows.
We were never their friend.

Plum Blossoms

The trees cause some anxiety,
vortexes sucking our attention from the road
as if rosy toddlers roamed the sidewalks.
They litter with everything they've got,
a storm of hats, gloves, pink bows,
fluffy toys blowing past.

This first disturbance
between winter and spring
holds out promises—we can repair
our mistakes; we can begin again—
and yanks them back
into fists of bark.

Those with sanguine attitude
picnic under blushy branches
where tiny particles of bee shit
fall on their heads. Like bees
they polish off the fodder
as if there were no tomorrow.

Instead of Thinking About Peaches

All those layers—
the seed's a bitter embryo inside
the lacework pit
woven among red tendrils close to the heart
the meat of the matter
the thick, sweet, dripping meat
we tear with our teeth, bruising and gouging
through delicate skin faintly brushed with fur
its tiny filaments funneling
and guiding the outer air around a perfect curve.

Left too long to its own devices
the fruit loses its grip and falls.
It bounces or splits or nestles in leaf litter,
softens, opens, gives itself up
to ants and multifarious bacteria.
I thought it would be easy
not to think
about a peach
and the way time eats us
or we rot.

Plant News

"The latest findings speak of a plant kingdom
brimming with chatter."
~Dan Cossins, *The Scientist*

The fennel grows jealous
of its space, stunting other plants.
The broad bean sends underground warnings
when blackflys swarm.

Lima beans eavesdrop—
they must know they're not popular.
Best friends basil and tomato push each other's growth.
In chemical language the messages never stop.

No one argues with the cedar
that spreads roots across the yard
leaving mere scraps of nutrients for the beans
and squash and not allowing any carrots at all.

Though I can't be sure, I believe I am kind
to the wild rose when I pinch off its dead blossoms
and clip the stems into order: it can't know
the consequences of roaming unchecked.

Life itself goes straggly that way,
nothing to show but thorns
and too many bare branches
vulnerable to herbivores and drought.

I've survived the drought of my life
by keeping my head down.
The fuchsia blooms facing earthwards
where it knows it will fall.

A Soldier in the Garden

In my garden I found a man
risen overnight with the peas.
Olive-green and the width of my thumb,
he wore goggles and helmet;
his hand curved empty where a weapon had been.
He had no feet, the breaking point
level and clean.

Last year I turned up a whiffle ball and resin frog
who'd burrowed among the roots
that thread this patch of dirt
like Sleeping Beauty's thorns gone under.

Sometimes the crows drop barter
for the dog treats or chicken scratch
I sprinkle in the grove,
leaving a shiny wrapper from the neighbor's garbage
or a broken pink clip.

I heard them muttering in the cedar
maybe watching me
take up this man
and put him down, half-buried
in the dust and quiet.

Heading indoors, I surprised a slug
waving his antennae insouciantly
as if I wouldn't notice
he'd ravaged the pansies
and clipped the buds off marigolds
like a child who'd disarm and dis-feet his toys.
I left his corpse for the crows to pick.

Dawn Redwood

Metasequoia glyptostroboides

On the highest tip-tilted stem of the dawn redwood
the Anna's hummingbird wheezes his song:
female wanted. Caught in direct light

he's mailed in green foil and an iridescent
violet cravat. His sleek grooming advertises wealth;
some girl will invite him home.

Worked threadbare, she'll raise the kids
while he's off to another family, still sporting that gloss.
When her children leave, she will get drunk on lavender.

We'll all get too old to fly. We want the flash, the style,
the exotic tree, sent as a wisp from China,
that now twists and reaches across the yard as if it owns the
    place.

I know the redwood feels some cellular triumph
every fall when it dumps its load of fronds and baubles
and every spring when it unfurls again,

marching smartly—in tree time—toward the house,
its system of veins, like mine, like the birds'
pumping the mysteries of air and soil.

One Tree, Three Stories

After the crows skim their portion of corn,
a squirrel twitches through the pine needles for leftovers,
tail yanking left and right, a critic.
Then the cleaners, dark-eyed juncos,
pick the last crumbs, leaving only chaff
for the ants and fungi. It sinks
into the bed of softening cellulose
where insects tunnel, food for kinglets'
quick, moss-green bounce to the highest tips.
A hard, sudden freeze knocks birds off branches.
If broken, the birds get on or die.
The crow missing a foot still hops and flies,
doesn't think about the meaning of wings,
glides in and out of the trees until he downs.
I don't know more than this.

The Frog Chorus

Love poems disguise
amphibian sex as sighs

deep stares, the ambivalent
human equivalent

of frogs clawing up the mud to toe height
powered by rising warmth and light

to state a single princely wish
to copulate with all whom they can catch.

How they go on, throats engorged with oxygen
mindlessly compelled to sing

and cast desire *basso profundo*
as far as sound will go

across the small domain that cups their lives,
getting lucky before they know love's died.

Disfluency

After great pain, a formal feeling ums.
Oh, I can't blame what's-her-name
for filling my days with misery,
her attention wandering from the few
yellow leaves still hanging from my
otherwise bare uh. You know
what they say about success counted sweetest
or was it something about loving well
what's going downhill
pretty soon. Anyway, we just couldn't get it
um, and don't most affairs end with a...?

Volatiles

> "As transferors of information, volatiles have provided
> plants with solutions to the challenges associated with
> being rooted in the ground."
> ~Ian T. Baldwin, "Plant Volatiles"

The orange nasturtium warns the yellow
of aphids, their black suede
covering its stems and the undersides of its platter-leaves.
Such generosity
is involuntary, I know,
a release of chemicals
through fungi connecting their roots
or air, an SOS to ladybugs
too late in summer for an answer.

Having landed here, you
get to know your dirt over the seasons.
You build soil with compost and mulch
and watch it flatten away again,
consumed by mysteries of plants and weather,
lazy worms or the cedar roots
sucking up your efforts.

There's comfort in routine
until a snowmelt or Biblical rain
reveals the bodies decomposing
just as they should,
greening the wasteland with guinea pigs and pet chickens,
the cat and the songbird she killed. In their volatiles
you breathe the endnote.

Rooted with them, a midden
of broken teacups, plastic arrows, one sandal, a flattened ball,
hieroglyphs telling a story of human lives beginning
and the need to plant ourselves
even as we disperse.

Shelley's Vegetables

"Percy Bysshe Shelley was a vegetarian and vegetarians
ought to make much of that fact by reading his poetic
and prose works."
~Reader Comment

A carrot keeps the good stuff
below the surface.
You never know what you'll find
inside a pea pod. Beware the worms;
they are meat.
Potatoes add gravitas to any dish.
As protean as the poet,
they accept all seasonings and
beaten, baked, boiled, whipped,
mashed, fried, they produce
an artful dinner. They deserve odes
like onions; read them
and weep. A memento mori, lettuce
begins to wilt as soon as picked;
but left in the ground, the leaves grow bitter.
In summer's heat, spinach transforms
like Daphne, into wood,
still alive
but unresponsive to our desire.
All make much of time
ere we make mush of them.

Variables

Summer begins with peas and ripens to peaches,
such bounty, such folly.

The concentration of bees on lavender and mint
gives way to wasps following me around the yard
as smarmy petitioners prod a squire
but light-fingered and carrying guns. Nobody wins.
I carry a stick
and break the webs in my path. No mercy.

A Northern Flicker attacks my roof—
pound, pound, pound and stop,
his halting synapses firing up: this
is not a tree. He launches with a wink of white feathers
but returns next day, having forgotten
he was here before.

In spring his clanging on the metal chimney
exaggerates his strength, warns other males
to give up without a fight.
But this is summer's end
when the nasturtiums twist into arthritic fingers
and the leaves of the wild rose pale to yellow.
We have no more chances.

Odonata

I don't know how it's possible—
tethered dragonflies
buzzing at the end
of their leads, dizzying, the circles
of them, the pricks of light
caught until they fall and fade.
Who could tie the threads
gently enough to restrain
yet not break a wing? Who
could catch an animal
with eyes like helmets
and a view in nearly every direction?

Underneath the iridescent motifs
on little girls' plastic purses and barrettes
they're a nightmare: spined legs and tarsal claws
hug close the prey as the mandible yawns
like an earth-mover's jaws and mashes its dinner's head.
They calculate distance, direction, and speed
of prey, their own angle of approach,
and snatch a fly mid-air before it knows
it has arrived where it was going.
How entomologists love their talent.

When you think they are hovering delicately
above the lily pads, wings glittering
and bodies flashing all the colors
of lust seen and unseen, they are hunting.
They dispense with courtship; it's grab and go
mid-air. Engineers deconstruct and copy
the four independent wings
but the materials stump them.
Odonata are already machines,
though we do not direct them. Best
to let them go, and follow.

Inertia

Though the fuss of leaves is gone from the dawn redwood,
branches still whisper with entangled birds
pecking the bobbled cones.

A caretaker of our parallel dimensions,
I crack ice in the birdbath; the cold snaps
at my bare fingers, the ends of me
shriveling like the daphne I nurtured from a slip.

I've left off trying to save her.

The sun never stirs above eye level,
its glare a taunt—somewhere it warms,
not here.

Where frozen mud has bubbled
only rocks flower, infertile bulbs
more numerous than birds, more lasting.

The unquiet mind may shift like gusted leaves
but settles to the same ruts.

Ice leaves an illusion of clarity
where the past, normally so slippery
with squashed intentions and the rotten fruit
of our labors, freezes in place

among the evergreens, a carnivore
ready to spring.

Two Crows

New to this place, I hear a crash
and see my neighbor loading his recycle bin
hidden from the street. Face set to his work
he doesn't see me at the kitchen sink

waiting for songbirds in the boundary trees.
Four months until leaves shelter
my yard; until then windows gape
straight through to my pantry's tumbled bags

of flour and almonds. I snaked the almonds
from fence to deck. Days passed
before the crows first ventured down
from the wire where they argued against the sky;

and now from their perch those corbies see
who steps out and who stays shuttered in,
the garbage lids shut firmly, the scavenging sparse
but for a compost heap concealed behind a wall,
a trail of seeds, a closing door.

The Certainty of the Anna's Hummingbird

Against the dirty clouds he's no bigger than a word
and the waves of his tinny chirp drift
across the yard before falling noiselessly,
dusting the bare lilac tree without waking it.
He does not know he can drop dead
at any moment. Nor do I, though I pretend
to imagine it for both of us. Each time
I step outside, I look for him. He has important work
just staying alive, keeping his carbon burning.

How can he be alive at all, a hummingbird in January
in the north where no flowers bloom
but the forced hyacinths and orchids behind glass
in our houses where they make a pretense of spring?
Perhaps a neighbor has put up a feeder of sugar-water;
perhaps my yard has such unbearable sweetness
that he cannot leave.

Part Three:
A Life That Big

Missouri River

This was alien country
flat as despair, stubbled, stripped
of atmosphere, sucking air from my throat,
turning my eyes to ice. We were as green
to each other as I to Nebraska

where I didn't comprehend Christmas morning,
summoned in pajamas as if one of the family
to tear into papers and boxes like dogs at a hen.
I lifted a red robe from white tissue
and hid in its folds.

Framed by the window, the river
congregated in tumbled chunks,
ice and snow without a shore-
line, bluing in low sun,
barely moving.

His dying mother, wigless,
wound her clock collection
in every room the ticking and cuckooing and cheeping and
        ringing
so that one hour was never divided from another
and time did not pass but continued
until everyone wore down and stilled in that frozen air.

Food Chain

"A scat study of wild snow leopards yielded the following annual menu per animal: five blue sheep, five domestic goats, one domestic sheep, marmots, nine Tibetan woolly hare, fifteen birds."
                    ~R.S. Chundawat, *Snow Line*

How many marmots?
Are they insignificant
or numberless like stars?
Humble, rounded rodents
of earth's upper crust,
they whistle an evensong
peak to peak.
The end of the day is coming,
the end, they say,
and the blue sheep
raise their heads from scrubby grass
and know it is time
to hide from leopards.

By tens and fifteens
marmots heap into burrows
for winter, squeezing past
and over each other,
casting pink litters
like grains of rice.
Biologists count all the snow leopards
in the world,
the number of goats in Tibet,
even the number of days
in one life.

They must guess at marmots
whose numbers ebb and flow
as seamlessly as seasons,
who sleep inside the earth
but are plucked like flowers
from the mountainside,
who know by shade of sky
and weight of air
that day is closing.
Then they sing.

I Announce the Dog's Birthday on Facebook

Friends, I would not name her *Shadow* or *Bear*
though she resembles a small bear when her fur grows out
in swirls around her body, and bears look like dogs
when their mouths are shut and their eyes peer kindly through
    the trees.

I do not prepare a ground turkey cake with cream cheese
    frosting
and *Emily* written in ketchup script. I do not admit
that I address her as Emily-Dear
or that I have written doggerel on her behalf.

I do not brush her teeth or clip her nails
as often as I should. I forget
she is outside on a cold day,
sitting quietly at the kitchen door while I write.

I have addressed her as Emma after a previous Airedale.
I have dragged her out from beneath my desk.
I have yelled at her when she ate the corners off my Persian rugs
which cost more than she did, which she did not know was
    wrong.

I am guilty of all the peccadillos of an imperfect guide
of her morality and mine. I am not her mom;
she is not my best friend. At night she guides
my breath; she sleeps in my husband's place.

When she looks into my face with unclouded dark eyes
traced in black like the portrait of an Egyptian goddess,
she is reading me to her advantage,
not to ask what she can do for me, her country,

but to know what she, the child of my choosing,
can expect from me next. She knows nothing
of birthdays, their celebratory pain leading
to repeated concussions of loss I invite again and again.

Metaphysic

I thank the neighbor's lilac tree
for lifting me along the trail of its perfume
with the scent I recall every winter as a longing for affection
that expands in the chest like breathing practice.

I thank the finches and chickadees
scoring their notes between the purple cones
while geraniums I buried last fall
crawl up green against the brown mulch.
I didn't know if they'd reignite
after months of drowning.

I praise them for returning, the dog for standing
here. I expect nothing.

Today the fighter jets fly out from their island, thunder muted
enough to pretend it's wind patting my house,
tickling the wind chime to call birds.
I'd select the bird with the sleekest feathers,
the one who looks after himself
and hangs upside-down to please me.

Outside our perfect circle and down the road,
my students rehearse locking doors and hiding behind desks.
Farther south, a volcano hibernates and contemplates
in geologic time when to bury its valley
of berries farmed for my Saturday market.

The earth's plates will give themselves
a hard shake like a dog after a bath
and the earth will crack and fold, the solid dirt
suddenly liquified or yawned open
and I would be one with the universe
although I would not know it.

We Were Girls

We swung ourselves bareback onto our bay horses,
left hand wrapped in the mane, right on the withers,
two steps and a leap into a western movie,
no faith in gravity or pain.

We'd take our horses into adulthood
and move to the barns we planned instead of weddings
which would take care of themselves
like school where we swung from one grade
to the next and landed safe.

We would buy Major, the tattered gray donkey
alone in his paddock
where we stopped to rub his jaw
and hold carrots and apples to his yellow teeth.
We beckoned his long ears with songs
while he and our horses breathed into each other

until we left.
His scream followed us—
a *Tekiah Gedolah* blast from the shofar,
a soul cut loose in space—
we always left.

Difficult Rocks

After the volcano lesson, rocks appeared
from our pockets, lunch bags and desks.
Igneous, said the geologist, *igneous, igneous*
—I thought ignoramus—
with bits of mineral packed like poppy seeds in bread,
glitters of mica, feldspar, olivine, hornblende,
spotted, streaked, coarse grained or smooth.
There was always a boy flashing a geode.

We set on their own shelf the not-rocks,
the concrete or slag disguised as rocks,
the fragments of brick or glass tumbled in a stream.
We can be fooled;
we can take one thing for another.

With a pyramid of quartz found in the lake
and kept in a jewelry box with a pop-up ballerina
spinning to Chopin until metal fatigue
dropped her sideways like a dying bug,
I held *conchoidal fracture, vitreous luster.*

From my house on the lake shore,
I watched the sleeping volcano
that held up the horizon,
its white snow veined in blue
like the rocks. It had flowered here once
and left behind the mysteries of form
in rocks rounding and tumbling under the waves.

Dry, the shoreline rocks dulled like winter sky
but in the water transformed
with washes of red and green,
minute crystals hinting of diamonds,
secret stories, children's stories—

The ballerina who danced herself to death,
the whale hoarding rocks and a wooden boy in its belly,
the witch who ate lost children,
the boys who urged us into the woods.
The lake sucked at my feet digging into the pebbles
and the long way they travelled to be here.

Set to Rights

The Skyhawk slipped through a hole in the firmament,
diving sharply before straightening its shoulders
and bouncing down the rutted road to a banana field
where it stopped, nosing the green fruit
as if ready to browse.
                              In a silence like listening
the four aboard sat for one full minute
unable to account for their lives.

                              The pilot thought
he might become a painter
and his wife thought the recurring dream of swimming
through leaves thrown open like arms
ended here
                              while the boy and girl in back
jumbled through broken bananas,
bruised knees, and bragging rights at school
and life resumed its going out and its coming in
and the oxen assumed their polished yokes and red embroidery
to pace the day's circles, wringing cane stalks dry.

The Way We Saw the Rabbit

The neighbor children jumped into my yard
and stumbled after the cottontail
    that, calculating speed and distance
as well as any software,
      waited,
      chewing mightily,
until they thought they had a chance of reaching it
         before it flashed into the trees,
    last to be seen
        not the white puff of tail
    but the back paddle-paws thrusting
    the sharp nails that would rake deep welts
on the children if they caught it.

I've heard the scream
    of a panicked rabbit
    kicking hard enough to break its spine.
        But today's marauder boldly goes
    and comes again to eat my snap peas and grass,
    his idyllic threat ended
    soon enough when a car or coyote snaps him away,
when the children turn to their screens
and forget this fantasy, the almost-touch,
    the hunger
that pulled them here.

Poem for a Jaded Appetite

This morning a lion
looks up from the rabbit she killed in your front yard.

You're surprised at the thickness of her paws,
the small, round ears. In truth, you're avoiding
her eyes—intent, pensive, you can't tell—and the crunching
noise penetrating the window.
Wrens dip overhead, *bonne bouche.*

When the sun lights your yard to the color of sand,
you think *lions of North Africa, Dido*
broken by a man heading for an empire
that didn't yet exist

instead of warning the neighbors
about keeping pets and children indoors.

Tidy as any housecat, she cleans teeth and paws.
Tufts of brown fur tumble across the yard.
You wonder about getting to your car
but idly, one part of your mind still teasing
at Dido and why she gave Aeneas
the kingdom she had built

and herself, until there was nothing left of her
but scraps for the pyre.

From the moment she met him, her fate locked in place
like that of all the women who loved post-war wanderers,
like her own warring selves,
the woman who birthed a country, the woman giving in.

The lion snugs under a rhododendron
for a nap. Let a neighbor call Fish and Wildlife;
you feel disinclined to upend the order of things.

Things That Are Made
to Be Knocked Down

When I say pink azalea
do you see magenta, coral, candy floss?
Don't look at the picture

which dabs this multi-hued plant
the color of cherry blossoms, sweet
but heartless—gone tomorrow.

An azalea isn't an azalea;
it's a rhododendron. You see
how difficult it is to communicate.

We both laughed at the counselor
shaking his fists: *so articulate,*
why can't you communicate with each other?

We should have confined our conversation
to the chickens, always getting loose
(your fault for not fixing the fence).

You translated the rooster's rich cluck—
here's a meaty bug—to reel in the hens
thinking *food* while he's thinking *fuck.*

Worked every time. Until the dog
killed the rooster. Do you see?

Erev Rosh Hashana

The forward motion of life
is ashes—the parrot who called my name
in my husband's voice, the man
himself, the berries that spoke
in our son's mouth, purple-black.

What I still have is the dying
angle of sunlight and the powdery warmth
of summer's end, the air
too sweet to leave for synagogue,
the child who shrank into a man.

The geese follow the same light,
carried on the same wind, this time
crying to me, *Can you follow your voice
into this emptiness and live?*

As It Is Said

We remember we were slaves.
The words rise in swirling columns
like the smoke and flames that guided us in circles
while we sustained ourselves with manna tasting like cornflakes
and believed we were headed somewhere.

We enact the parting of the Red Sea in Jello
and hurry little plastic figures across the tray.
Though we lost Pharaoh over the years,
we still have men in kilts to drown in the red glop.
We do not rejoice
at the deaths of our enemies.

Whatever happened 3,000 years ago
happened yesterday.
Everything means something else:
salt water, our tears when we were slaves,
horseradish for the bitterness of those days,
a cup of wine for the prophet Elijah, fleet-footed Mercury
who never shows up.

Everyone gets peckish enough to eat bitter herbs
before the sweet mortar of apples, nuts, and wine.
We built this house
to last, though much of the family has dropped by the wayside
during our lifetimes wandering from one Seder to another.
It is said
a generation had to die
before another without slave-minds
could build Jerusalem.
We thought arrival was enough.

Indian Ocean, Perth

Here it is, she said, sweeping her arm
as if opening a door to a guest room
primped with pillows and yellow sun

On this blank page of beach
without shells or kelp
we were two brushstrokes
on gray water, white sky

When I stepped in
the ocean tasted my feet,
the edge of the continent

I was twenty; I could imagine
four thousand miles to Madagascar
a life that big

Kodiak Moment

Today a bear will rise from the dead.
From a pile of bones, baked dry as dust
and disinfected, protected with
preservative and reconnected
she will emerge as large as life,
one paw with every finger bone
perfected reaching to pluck a plastic
salmon off its plinth, the mystery,
the labyrinth of bone made live,
solved before your very eyes.

Imagine your forebears reappearing thus,
propped by the door, robed in memory
but otherwise anonymous.
Children, this is immortality.

Acceptable Losses

"The state has boosted cougar hunting, despite a drop in
complaints, including sightings in residential areas and
livestock kills."
~*Seattle Times*

No one ever saw a cougar
on Cougar Way, the street bisecting
the town center and wandering into the territory
where children play in roads without fear of predators.

When the houses came, predators moved up the mountains
away from the streets bordering rows of houses
with pets and trash locked up at night.
Only the lost wander down.

Young cougars wander in search of new territory
beyond the marks and scrapes of older males.
If the urine's fresh, they move on;
if old, they might settle into the space left by absence.

Cougars are mostly absence
invisible in the roughest places where we do not wander,
where elk and deer climb high
outside the spreading territory we mark as ours.

The cougars who wander into our towns
or slip through a back yard at dusk
are boys who know no better,
like the ones who drive too fast or dive into summer lakes
without looking ahead,

the ones who light out for the territory ahead
of the rest. Some make their mark, get rich.
Some become absence, wandering past
every border that would turn them, never home.

There I Am

sitting in the back yard
my four feet planted neatly in a square
in the gloaming when everything is washed violet
and a gold gleam still knifes across the horizon
when you can't be sure that what you see
is what you see
and I am at the kitchen window watching
myself sitting
head raised to the crows
streaming like soot on their way to roost
sniffing the currents and not thinking
of anything but the stories
told by scents tunneling along my snout
the heather blooming and the trails of chickens
climbing into their barn as the warmth leaves
as it always does
everything
settling into its place
for just a second all is well
and I do not mind being alone forever

Wild Speculations

"... the writings of the plant neurobiologists suffer from
'over-interpretation of data, teleology, anthropomorphizing,
philosophizing, and wild speculations.'"

~Lincoln Taiz

If the spearmint would confine itself
to the pot and not slither across the patch
shared with oregano and calendula,
we'd have no mid-summer brawl,

strangulation, chemical warfare,
roots pushing and shoving like third-grade boys
who do not understand
no one wins.

Some roots, sensing an impenetrable barrier,
(the side of a ceramic pot) change direction
to follow the yielding soil, the nutrients;
but the mint has to be a cowboy.

Fixed to my house and worldly goods,
wanting more
than rain and nitrogen,

I do not claim plants make decisions
or deliberately invade one another's territory.
Though they occupy most of the earth
and we animals are mere trace minerals,
plants lack neurons.

The mint lacks regret when it dies back in winter;
only I mourn its leaves' lost companionship
for my bourbon. While the mint sleeps,

[...]

I tear its runners out of the soil
and tuck the rest safely back in the pot.

It wakes in spring, stretches.
A natural speculator,
it might go anywhere.

A Day of Good News

I raked the wet apple-leaves into the hen yard
where the young chickens prowled around the pile,
suspicious of this new thing

until the boldest, the chestnut tinted Rhode Island Red
picked at a leaf, dropped it, lifted a minute bug,
stepped forward, followed by the other three

and then began their dance of foot forward and pulling back
head dipping for larvae and woodlice,
the hidden eggs of slugs and millipedes
forward, back, peck, muttering and singing to each other

until all the leaves were spread across the pen
as they had been over the lawn;
now each one examined and plucked clean,
a tablecloth of gold and brown covering the mud
churned now with manure, food for microbes

that will pick apart the fabric
and leave lacework skeletons and leaf mold
for worms to weave through their veiny tunnels in the soil—
the red hen and black, the tan and ochre
turning and turning the leaves, not attending
to the misty rain laying over us a beadwork like crystal.

– Acknowledgments –

With thanks to the publications in which the following poems previously appeared:

Cider Press Review: "This Time of Year," "A Day of Good News"

Charles River Review: "Tuning," "A History of Glass"

Cirque Journal: "Wildlife Rescue"

Cloudbank: "Acceptable Losses," "The Distance," "Turkey Vultures"

Clover: "Miss Sarah Stone Records Natural Curiosities from the New World," "Tell the Bees"

Cold Creek Review: "Missouri River"

Connecticut River Review: "I announce the dog's birthday on Facebook"

Crosswinds Poetry Journal: "Odonata," "Plum Blossoms," "The Moment He Leaves My Hands"

Dandelion Review: "Linnaeus Names Andromeda"

Forgotten Women (anthology): "Sarah Stone Paints the O'o Bird"

Kettle Blue Review: "Set to Rights"

Marathon Literary Review: "Properties of Glass"

Miramar: "Erev Rosh Hashana"

Pink Panther: "The Newly Bereaved Fixes a Toilet," "We Were Girls"

Poetry Northwest: "Difficult Rocks"

Poor Yorick: "Stones Fall from the Sky"

Puerto del Sol: "Food Chain," "Kodiak Moment"

Raven Chronicles: "Biblical Summer," "There Will Be No Revolution"

Sand Hills Literary Review: "A Soldier in the Garden"

Sharkreef Review: "The Certainty of the Anna's Hummingbird," "The Misnomer Renaissance Faire," "Two Crows"

Star 82 Review: "Disfluency"

Tar River Review: "The Body Falls Away"

The Sow's Ear Poetry Review: "Slip," "The Fly-Out," reprint of "Odonata"

The Timberline Review: "Storm Season," "Variables"

Watershed Review: "Norway Lemmings," "Sea Turtle at Tortuguero, Costa Rica"

Waypoint: "If I Could"

Weatherbeaten: "Reseeded Lawn"

"Food Chain" and "Kodiak Moment" also appeared in the chapbook, *A Natural History of Grief*.

Thanks also to fellow poets Anne Pitkin, Alicia Hokanson, Eileen Duncan, and Mercedes Lawry whose tea, chocolate, and considerable intellect helped me prod many of these poems into shape.

– Citations –

Baldwin, Ian T., "Plant Volatiles," *Current Biology*, Vol. 20, No. 9, p. 392

Cossins, Dan, "Plant Talk," *The Scientist*, Jan. 1. 2014. https://www.the-scientist.com/features/plant-talk-38209

Curtin, Ciara "Fact or Fiction? Glass is a (Supercooled) Liquid," *Scientific American*, Feb. 22, 2007.

Marzorati, Gerald, "Better Aging Through Practice, Practice, Practice," *New York Times*, April 29, 2016

Taiz, Lincoln as quoted by Michael Pollan in "The Intelligent Plant," *The New Yorker*, Dec.15, 2013. https://www.newyorker.com/magazine/2013/12/23/the-intelligent-plant

Young, C. Dale, "Few Shall Answer," *Slate*, April 26, 2005. https://slate.com/culture/2005/04/few-shall-answer.html

Zagajewski, Adam "The Revolution Has Ended," *Unseen Hand*, Clare Cavanagh, translator Farrar Straus Giroux, New York, 2011

– Praise for –
Between States of Matter

Nothing stays at rest, writes Sherry Rind, and, indeed, these are restless poems—probing, examining, taking nothing for granted—by a poet who is not fooled by easy appearances. There is an edge to Rind that has been honed on the worn stone of experience, the relentless strop of memory. Still, she finds solace in the adaptability of wild animals, insects, birds, the fierce allegiance of dogs and the tenacity of plants. She is, finally, a poet of hope, one who has been able to, as Wendell Berry says, *Be joyful/ though you have considered all the facts.*

~Samuel Green, Inaugural Poet Laureate, Washington State

Traversing a tightrope of grief and loss, Sherry Rind's *Between States of Matter* blends exquisite imagery with explorations of science and art. These poems reach widely through history and literature to capture Darwin, Sarah Stone, and Percy Bysshe Shelley. Though mortality is never far away, the organic force of life and living comes to the fore: *He has important work/just staying alive,/ keeping his carbon burning.* Rind is a gardener steeped in the natural world: *The mint lacks regret when it dies back in winter;/ only I mourn its leaves' lost companionship/ for my bourbon.* There is an edge to her verse—a poignant music that captures the stillness between what we long to catch hold of and what's inevitably lost.

~Judith Skillman, author of *Came Home to Winter*

The poems in this new collection proliferate with imagery in motion between states of being—flora and fauna domestic and wild, and constant shifts and transitions in their natural history. There are vegetable gardens and suburban lawns to be cared for, exotic and extinct birds and their lore preserved by collectors, sea turtles hauling up between sand and sea to lay their eggs, adolescent cougars prowling human neighborhoods in the interface zones at the edges of former wilderness. All of this richness is refracted through the poems' prevailing subject—the awareness of life's evanescence made acute by loss and its lifelong burden of grief. Many of these poems deliver quiet epiphanies, a flash of uplifting or devastating insight at the end: *when the great joints of the earth/ begin to shift against their sockets./ All our work will be undone.* Dwelling in a state between states, Rind invites us to contemplate how *time refracts everyone's history* and to enter these poems like light passing through the ever-shifting *gather of glass.*

~Carolyne Wright,
author of *This Dream the World: New & Selected Poems,*

– About the Author –

Granddaughter of immigrants, Sherry Rind takes her chances with poetry instead of crossing the Atlantic with a few *biscochos* by way of kosher food. She published her first poems when still in college. Earning her BA in a recession, she decided the only solution was to return to school, working as a teaching assistant and earning her MA in advanced writing. She taught writing at community colleges and for arts commissions, and worked in development and at miscellaneous other jobs, as writer do.

She received grants and awards from the Seattle and King County Arts Commissions, Pacific Northwest Writers, National Endowment for the Arts, and Artist Trust. She edited two books about Airedale terriers and published numerous articles about parrots. She has published two chapbooks, *The Whooping Crane Dance* and *A Natural History of Grief*, runner-up for the Quentin R. Howard Chapbook Prize. Her books are *The Hawk in the Back Yard*, winner of the Anhinga award and published by Anhinga Press, and *A Fall Out the Door*, winner of the King County Arts Commission Publication Award and published by Confluence Press. She has always lived with multiple animals and knows she is one.

– About The Poetry Box –

The Poetry Box® is a boutique publishing company that enjoys providing a platform for both established and emerging poets to share their words with the world through beautiful printed books and chapbooks.

Feel free to visit the online bookstore (thePoetryBox.com), where you'll find more titles including:

November Quilt by Penelope Scambly Schott

Shrinking Bones by Judy K. Mosher

Small Blue Harbor by Ahrend Torrey

Impossible Ledges by Dianne Avey

Bee Dance by Cathy Cain

Like the O in Hope by Jeanne Julian

Shadow Man by Margaret Chula

What She Was Wearing by Shawn Aveningo Sanders

A Long, Wide Stretch of Calm by Melanie Green

Moroccan Holiday by Lauren Tivey

Hello, Darling by Christine Higgins

Falling into the River by Debbie Hall

Notes from a Caregiver by Meg Lindsay

and more . . .

CPSIA information can be obtained
at www.ICGtesting.com
Printed in the USA
FSHW021315260220
67460FS